W9-ATR-726

Beginning to END

Milk

To

Ice Cream

A Buddy Book

by

Julie Murray

ABDO
Publishing Company

VISIT US AT
www.abdopublishing.com

Published by ABDO Publishing Company, 4940 Viking Drive, Edina, Minnesota 55435.

Printed in the United States.

Coordinating Series Editor: Sarah Tieck
Contributing Editor: Michael P. Goecke
Graphic Design: Maria Hosley
Cover Photograph: Media Bakery
Interior Photographs/Illustrations: Media Bakery, Photos.com, Photodisc
Special thanks to the Humboldt Creamery for use of photos.

Library of Congress Cataloging-in-Publication Data

Murray, Julie, 1969–
    Milk to ice cream / Julie Murray.
        p. cm. — (Beginning to end)
    Includes index.
    ISBN-13: 978-1-59679-838-0
    ISBN-10: 1-59679-838-6
    1. Ice cream, ices, etc.—Juvenile literature. 2. Ice cream industry—Juvenile literature. 3. Milk—Juvenile literature. I. Title.

TX795.M87 2006
637'.4—dc22

                                                                2006019896

Table Of Contents

Where Does Ice Cream Come From? 4

A Starting Point 8

Fun Facts 10

The Milking Process 12

From Cow To Cone 15

Can You Guess? 22

Important Words 23

Web Sites 23

Index 24

Where Does Ice Cream Come From?

Many people like to eat ice cream. They eat it on cones or in dishes. And sometimes, they add toppings such as hot fudge or whipped cream.

Ice cream comes in many different flavors. New ice creams are created all the time.

There are simple ice cream flavors, such as chocolate, vanilla, and strawberry. There are also flavors with chunks of sweets mixed in. These flavors include rocky road, mint chocolate chip, and cookie dough.

Some ice creams are flavored with fruit.

Ice cream is a dairy product. This means it is made from milk.

Milk comes from cows. Cows live on farms around the world. Do you know how your favorite kind of ice cream is made?

Cows that are raised to make milk are called dairy cows.

A Starting Point

Milk is a **natural** product that comes from a cow's body. A female cow's body makes milk after she has a baby. A baby cow is called a calf.

A calf drinks milk from its mother's udder. An udder is where a cow's milk is made and stored. It hangs down near a cow's back legs. Cows can produce as much as 10 gallons (38 l) of milk every day.

Farmers can collect and sell a cow's milk.

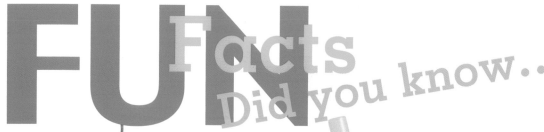

FUN Facts
Did you know...

Yum!

… A man named Jacob Fussell opened the first commercial ice cream factory in 1851.

… In 1744, Governor Thomas Bladen of Maryland was one of the first people to serve ice cream at a dinner party.

cream

cookie

cookies & cream ice cream

... Cookies and cream ice cream was invented in 1983. It quickly became one of the top-selling ice cream flavors. Another popular flavor is cookie dough. This started selling in 1991.

cookie dough

cookie dough ice cream

... In 1776, the first ice cream parlor in the United States opened in New York City.

vanilla ice cream

The Milking Process

Farmers must milk cows in order to get their milk. Some farmers milk cows by hand. But, most farmers use milking machines. Dairy cows are milked twice each day.

A milking machine squeezes a cow's teats.

To milk a cow by hand, a farmer squeezes the **teats** on the cow's udder. This makes the milk squirt out. Milking machines use a similar process to get a cow's milk.

Farmers store milk in special tanks. These tanks keep milk cold so it doesn't spoil. Spoiled milk could make people sick.

Later, a truck picks up the cold milk from the dairy farm. The truck delivers the milk to a **factory** called a dairy. Milk that is going to be made into ice cream is then delivered to an ice cream factory.

Dairy trucks have a special tank that keeps milk cool.

From Cow To Cone

Machines at an ice cream **factory** make ice cream. Many machines are used during this process. The first machine is the mixing tank. This is where ice cream **ingredients** are mixed together.

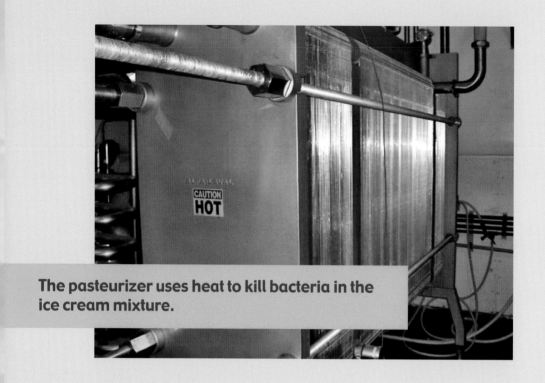

The pasteurizer uses heat to kill bacteria in the ice cream mixture.

Next, the mixture is heated in a pasteurizer. This process helps clean the ice cream mixture by killing **bacteria**. This makes the ice cream safe for people to eat.

The next machine is called a homogenizer. This machine uses a lot of **pressure** and weight to break down milk fat. This part of the process makes the ice cream smooth and creamy.

The homogenizer helps give ice cream its smooth texture.

After the homogenizing process, the ice cream mixture is cooled. It is then placed in a special freezer. There, blades whip the mixture while it is freezing. This mixes air into the ice cream.

Before the ice cream goes to the last freezer, flavorings and **ingredients** are added. These foods often include fruit, cookies, or chocolate chips.

Ice cream factories have more than one freezer. When making ice cream, there are a couple stages in the freezing process.

Freshly packed ice cream containers move through the factory on a conveyor belt.

Before ice cream is frozen solid, it is packaged into containers. Then, it is placed in a hardening room. When the ice cream is frozen solid, it is taken to stores. Then, people can buy it!

Next time you eat a bite of ice cream, be sure to think about its journey from cow to cone!

Ice cream goes through many processes before people can enjoy eating it.

Can You Guess?

Q: Which First Lady served ice cream in the White House in 1812?

A: Dolly Madison. It was the dessert at the inaugural ball.

Q: When was the ice cream cone invented?

A: Many people say it happened at the 1904 World's Fair in St. Louis, Missouri. Legend says that a man selling ice cream ran out of bowls. So, he teamed up with a person selling waffles. They combined the two ideas to make the first waffle cones.

Important Words

bacteria very small organisms that can grow in food and other places. Bacteria can make people sick.

factory a business that uses machines to help with work.

ingredient a part of a mixture.

natural from nature.

pressure the force applied to help move something.

teat the part of an udder where milk comes out.

Web Sites

To learn more, visit ABDO Publishing Company on the World Wide Web. Web site links about this topic are featured on our Book Links page. These links are routinely monitored and updated to provide the most current information available.

www.abdopublishing.com

Index

bacteria 16

Bladen, Thomas 10

calf 8

cones 4, 20, 22

cow 6,
7, 8, 9, 12, 13, 15, 20

dairy 6, 7, 12, 14

dish 4

factory 10,
14, 15, 19, 20

farm 6, 14

farmer 9, 12, 13, 14

flavors 4, 5, 11, 18

freeze 18, 19, 20

Fussell, Jacob 10

ingredients 5, 15, 18

machine 12,
13, 15, 16, 17, 18, 19

Madison, Dolly 22

Maryland 10

Missouri 22

New York City 11

tank 13, 14, 15

United States 11

White House 22

World's Fair 22